D0941175

"It is one thing to photograph people. It is another to make others care about them by revealing the core of their humanness."

Paul Strand, Photographer

To Mattaya and Benjamin,
my favourite little humans in the entire universe.

First Edition

Humans of Nelson
Author and Photographer: Ryan Oakley, ryanoakleyphotography.ca
Project Consultant: Anne Degrace, annedegrace.ca
Layout and Design: Steven Cretney, theforest.ca
Photographic Post Production: Derek Bisbing, hugephotography.com
Text set in Calluna Sans

Printed and bound in Canada by Friesens Printers, an FSC certified printer. Printed on
recycled, FSC certified paper with vegetable/soya based inks.

Oakley, Ryan (Ryan Christopher), 1978-, author
    Humans of Nelson / Ryan Oakley.

ISBN 978-0-9939100-0-5 (bound)

    1. Nelson (B.C.)--Pictorial works. 2. Portrait photography--
British Columbia--Nelson. I. Title.

FC3849.N44O23 2014   971.1'62   C2014-906095-5

HUMANS

_of_

NELSON

Ryan Oakley

Introduction

To understand the Humans of Nelson project, I need to first talk about the Humans of New York, created by photographer Brandon Stanton.

Brandon began by travelling around US cities photographing anything and everything he saw. When he got to a new place, he'd create a Facebook album where he would document his impressions. Pittsburg was yellow steel bridges; Philadelphia was bricks and flags. When Brandon arrived in New York, his first impression was the people—and Humans of New York was born.

He began posting photos, then added anecdotes and quotes—things people said that were interesting or poignant or funny. Now, Humans of New York is an internet sensation, followed and loved by millions of people around the world.

When a friend sent me a link to Humans of New York I was instantly captivated. Within an hour I discovered there were spin-off projects in cities around the world. And I learned that Brandon gave these photographers his blessing.

I held my breath and did an internet search for Humans of Nelson, BC. Nothing! So before I could talk myself out of it, I took the leap: I registered the humansofnelsonbc.ca website and created the Facebook page. But did I have it in me to ask a stranger if I could take their photograph? That same day I went out on the street with my camera, my heart pounding.

The first person I asked said: "No, thanks."

The rejection didn't kill me (as I thought it might). I tried again—and the next person said yes. I think I just stared at him. Then I remembered I had asked to take his picture. I brought the camera to my eye and pressed the shutter release. Nothing happened; I had forgotten to turn the camera on. Finally, I snapped one. Then I think I bolted. We didn't talk, and I can't remember if I told him thanks. (Thanks first person!) But at least now, I knew I could do it.

I shoot mostly on my lunch breaks from my day job as an engineer. I almost always have my camera with me. Sometimes I manage to talk myself out of shooting (it's too cold, they'll all say no, you'll embarrass yourself). But I've learned to embrace my fears and mute the voices. I tell myself: "Go shoot—you never know what amazing person you will meet today." Then I pick up my camera and head outside.

Nelson is an incredible place. I'm not originally from here, which I think helps me appreciate the gem it really is. I cherish it; I'm proud of it. When I have a free day, I might be found at Oso Negro with friends or reading a book, or strolling on Baker Street wondering if it's time to eat (the food here is so good). And I'll be watching the people, marvelling at how Nelson embraces it all. We love the colourful, the playful, the hitchhikers, the professionals, the families. In my mind, it's a tiny New York.

With this project, I've tried to get closer to the heart and spirit of Nelson. I stop strangers on the street, take their pictures, talk to them, and record some of the conversation. But flip through the book and you'll see it's more than that. There's the range of human experience in this collection. One moment you'll empathize with someone's sad story, but turn the page and you might laugh at something that's really silly.

You'll see that we're really not all that different from one another, and yet we are all unique. I hope you enjoy the Humans of Nelson as much as I have.

"May I take your photo?"

"Maybe. What's it for?"

"I run a site called Humans of Nelson."

"And what if I'm not human?"

"I'll bend the rules, this one time."

"OK. I'll stand here so you can get that awesome building in the background."

We talked for more than half an hour. We shared our stories. And by the end of it we were both almost in tears. I have four pages of notes from our conversation. But this is all I'm called to share:

"There's no shame in falling apart."

"I started sewing when I was 12. As I grew up I just kinda stopped. When my sister died nine years ago, I was depressed for a whole year after. It was really hard. Then I started to sew again. And the colours and creativity just bursted out of me. I attribute what I am able to make to my sister and her passing. Sewing healed me and now I get to share it with others."

"What's something you're struggling with?"

After a long pause – "Well, I'm having trouble coming up with an answer for that. It's a challenge for me. But that's good and I want to stay in that question for a minute."

"OK. I'm finding there is just so much opportunity out there. Everything that I want to manifest is appearing all around me. Like 360 degrees. So I'll be going down one path – trusting it... but then something else shows up. And I don't know if that's the universe testing my resolve on the first thing, or giving me a new direction I'm supposed to follow. I suppose clarity is the thing I'm struggling with right now."

"Happiest moment? Well, I try to be happy all the time. I like to smile. I think it's neat that it can help make someone's day. Like the other day I smiled at a stranger on the street. No reason. Just did it. But later that afternoon he saw me working at the Co-op and actually went out of his way to tell me that the smile I gave him earlier helped him form a positive impression of this town. That was pretty cool. From what I know, no harm can come from a smile."

After we talked about her hat, she told me she was thinking of moving to Nelson and wanted to know why Nelson would be better than the other ski towns she was considering. I told her that Nelson is so difficult to physically get to that the people that live here have generally made a sacrifice to make it happen. So those that are here, are happy to be here. And happy people make for a great community and place to live. In other words, very few Nelsonites are "stuck" here, like many others are stuck in big cities for various reasons: family, jobs, school.

What's funny looking back at that conversation is I said nothing about the quality of skiing.

"My name is Jan...Maggie"

"I'm sorry, did you just almost call yourself Jan and then changed your mind to Maggie?"

"Well, sort of. I changed my name two years ago."

"Why?"

"I grew up with the name Jan. That's what my adoptive parents called me. Then a little while ago I found out my birth mother called me Maggie. Maggie felt more 'me', you know?"

"Of course. Nice to meet you Maggie."

"My father never had respect for me growing up. He was a conventional, military, religious man. Everything was black and white, and I didn't fit his mold. We had no closeness; no attempt was made to try to understand each other. And I can never remember him saying 'I love you'. We stopped talking for 45 years. I lived my life and he lived his.

Time passed. He got old. He got sick.

I decided to love him anyways and I took care of him in his final years. In the end he loved me and told me so. I'm glad I didn't wait for him to come to me."

The lady on the right and I were talking. It was just us at first.
And it was difficult because I couldn't explain the Humans of
Nelson project to her well enough for her to understand and be
comfortable answering my questions.

Sometimes it happens that people get uncomfortable and
instead of pressing to get a good quote, I just simply thank them
for their time and willingness and I move on.

And I was about to do just that when the woman on the left
showed up. "I'm sorry, am I interrupting something?"

I briefly introduced myself and explained what I was doing. At
which point I repeated the question I had asked the other lady,
"If you could give a piece of advice to a large group of people,
what would it be?"

The woman on the left turned to the lady on the right and said
"Smile and be happy!" And that's when I realized that ever since
this new person showed up, the lady on the right had become
comfortable and was just beaming at the woman on the left.

"And you are?"

"Her mom."

"What's your favourite thing about your mom?"

"Last night she taught me how to use the turntable."

"I've seen a lot of communities ruined by progress."

"What's the answer?"

"I don't know. But I think it has to start with affordable housing."

"I'm having a tough time figuring out how I'm going to go from school – where all I'm doing is sitting down, sitting still, and doing what I'm told – to becoming an adult where I know I'll need to take full control of my life."

"So you're scared of that transition?"

"No. I'm excited."

"You're the only one I've seen so far today walking around with an old ukulele, missing a string."

"Ha! I just picked this up from my grandma. She gave it to me. It was hers when she was a teenager. I've always wanted it. I'm on my way to get a new string for it."

"Do you mind if I try it out?"

"Sure!"

I then played the only riff I knew how to play on the ukulele. I was sure she would recognize it as the intro to a popular Nirvana song. After 30 seconds of me playing the notes on repeat, I looked up at her and it was clear she had no idea what song I was playing.

I was flustered. I was expecting applause – or something. When she asked me what song it was, I was at a loss to remember the name of it. What I thought would be an epic moment turned out to be pretty lame. I hope she does better with the instrument than I did.

"What's the best thing about having a kid?"

"I get to see life through her eyes. It keeps me young."

"What's the hardest part?"

"None of my friends have kids."

"What was the best thing that happened to you last year?"

"I moved back to Nelson!"

"How long had you been away?"

"20 years. I always knew I would come back, I just didn't think it would take so long. But now I'm just so grateful. I have a good job, a good home. It all came together and I couldn't be happier."

"I'm big into symbols and stuff. I'm wearing things that mean something to me. Things in my hair, my bracelets – lots of them have stories and memories they're attached to. It's like I'm wearing what most people put in their diary. It's all here, a part of me. I can look at something and not only remember what happened, why I have it, but also all the emotions that go with it too."

"Can you show me something that has a story attached to it?"

"This bracelet here, that my first boyfriend gave to me. And this one I made – it's for my first love. I made one for him too. It used to have a bead on it but it fell off right when I got over our relationship. I love the coincidence and serendipity of that."

"If you could give a piece of advice to a large audience, what would it be?"

"Oh, I don't know. Keep breathing."

"OK. Anything else?"

"Learn to release anything in your life that doesn't serve you. If you can do that, you remove your own victimhood out of the situation. My view on life is that everything we encounter is a reflection of everything that we are. So with that, we should be grateful for everything that happens – good and bad. Because either way, that's what's teaching us about ourselves. We just need to pay attention. And keep breathing."

"I'm looking for a job. But I'll find one – I just have to stay positive."

UPDATE: He's got a job!

"What's something you're struggling with right now?"

"Letting people be people. We don't need to control each other.
We don't all need to believe the same things to be friends."

I saw this guy sitting just outside of John Ward Coffee. We made eye contact and before I could ask to take his photo, he says "Hey man. Wanna hug?" "Of course!" I replied.

He leapt out of his chair and we embraced. Man to man, stranger to stranger, human to human. Completely out of the blue. I'd never met or seen this guy before that moment.

After the hug and the more regular exchange of pleasantries I asked him if I could take his photo. He was a bit reluctant. But his hesitation lasted just three seconds before he started striking these epic poses on the sidewalk. My trigger finger couldn't keep up! He was all over the place. One pose after another.

Finally, he gave me the time-out "T" with his hands indicating the shoot was officially over. I was stunned. "That was AWESOME. Now do you mind if I ask you a few questions? I'd like to add something about you to the photo."

"Do you mind if I ask *you* a question?"

"Sure. What is it?"

"What's your favourite fruit?"

Damn. This guy is good.

"I was in a motorbike accident 40 years ago. I spent 597 days in the hospital. This is my fourth hip replacement and I've had my ankle fused twice. As you get older, your body degrades and we all have to deal with not being able to do the things we did when we were younger. But if you're already degraded like me, the aging process is much worse."

"Do you still ride?"

"Hell ya."

"Do you write your own songs?"

"Of course I can... but I don't."

"Why not?"

"When you've been roommates with Willie P. Bennett and Joni Mitchell's drinkin' buddy, you get humble."

I asked them if they had any ideas for posing.

They said sure and then did this...

"Many years ago, I fell and injured my head. It took me a while to even figure out that something was wrong. I kept forgetting things...but I thought I was just getting old."

"What's it like living with a head injury?"

"It's actually not that bad. My life is pretty simple. I get peace and quiet - and lots of time to commune with myself. I even get these really vivid memories of my childhood. Out of nowhere things will pop in my head and I'll even experience the emotion of the memory."

"And what's the hardest part?"

"When I'm in the middle of saying something important and the next word or sentence just leaves my mind. Poof. But if I'm patient, the thought will come back – just not always when I want it to."

"What's something you're struggling with right now?"

"The weariness of being embodied in such a slow form of energy."

"What do you mean?"

"Rocks would have a slow energy, right? They take so much time and pressure to change. The sun has fast energy. It's explosive. Our bodies, our bones, have such a slower energy than our thoughts – which is our fastest form. Every morning I wake up and I'm surprised that I'm still in this body. It's part of the struggle, but it's also part of the fun."

"Long lineup at the dentist office today. Who's up next?"

"I think the hippo."

Best. Shirt. Ever.

"What's your biggest regret?"

"Having my first drink."

"What's your favourite thing about him."

"His smile. He's a very happy kid."

"What's something he does that makes him really happy?"

"He loves to ride our dog like a horse."

"I want to teach young kids."

"What's your biggest struggle right now?"

"I have some tough decisions to make coming up. Do I take the job that pays the most but takes me away from where I want to be? Or do I stay and do something I enjoy that pays less?"

"What would you do that you enjoy?"

"Tree planting. I love it."

"Sounds like an easy choice."

"Yeah, I'll probably take the job that pays more."

"You want a story? No, I don't have any stories... maybe just that
I've survived two plane crashes."

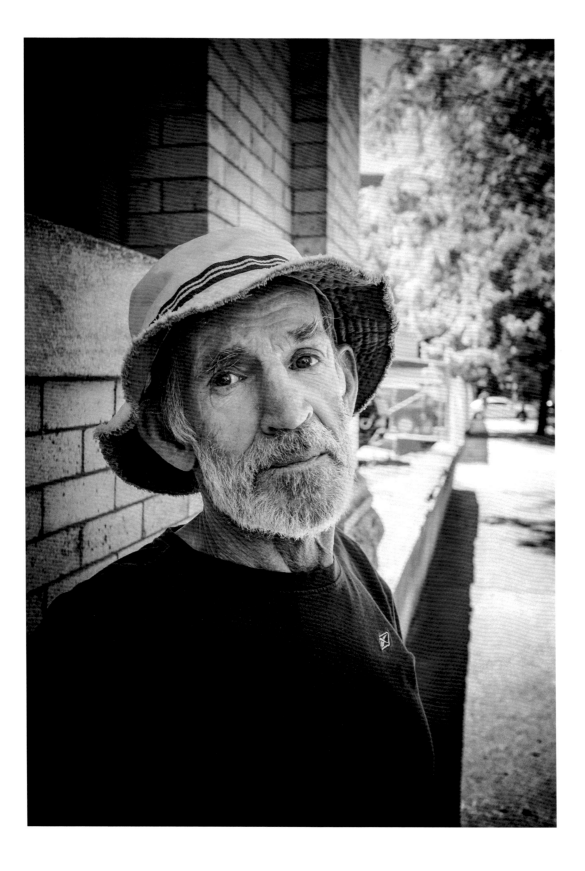

"Oh I don't know. I don't have anything to share."

"Tell me something you are passionate about."

"I like to draw."

"And what do you draw?"

"Whatever the pencil tells me to. I just let it do what it wants. It almost always starts with an eye and then goes from there. Maybe it turns into a flower. Or into something else. I don't know why."

I offered her my notebook and pen that I always carry around with me. I asked if she could draw me something. The only room I had left was on the last page – which was ripped in half. But somehow that felt like a great canvas – to me, anyways.

When she was finished I asked her to sign and date it. She looked at me like I was crazy and told me it was just a doodle and it wasn't very good. I told her that I loved it and I was very thankful that she took the time to make it for me.

The magic that goes on in this shop never fails to impress me and my inner five year-old.

"The end is nigh. Don't be afraid. The Spirit will carry us home."

"I took Wings Grocery over from my brother who retired and moved back to Vancouver two years ago. We switched places. He moved from here to Vancouver, and I moved from Vancouver to Nelson."

"What did you do before owning Wings? Did you own another store like this one?"

"No, no. I used to make models."

"Models of what? Planes?"

"Ha ha. No. Buildings. Like show homes."

"Like the one for the Nelson Commons housing development."

"Yes exactly. I did that."

"You did models like that."

"No. I built *that* model. The one of the new development in Nelson. I built it before I came here."

"Holy crap. Really?"

"Yes."

"If I'm not creating, I'm not happy. If I'm not around plants, I'm not happy. Thankfully, I work as a floral designer."

Seen in an alley.

"Excuse me, do you mind if I take your picture?"

"Oh. Yeah. Sure. You look just like the electrician that came by my house yesterday."

"Did he do good work?"

"Yeah, but the fan over my stove is too loud now."

"If I see someone that looks like me, I'll let him know."

"How long have you two been friends?"

"Well...it's been umpteen years."

"What's kept your friendship strong for umpteen years?"

"Oh, I don't know. She's just so special to me."

"Do you recall the saddest moment of your life?"

"I don't have sad moments."

"None?"

"No. I don't believe in sad moments."

"Do you like bears?"

"........"

"Do you like bear hugs from your mom?"

"........"

"Are you a bit shy?"

"........"

"Thanks for letting me take your photo."

"You're welcome."

"What advice would you give a large group of people?"

"Stay away from religion. I spent my childhood sitting on a hard wooden bench being told to be quiet. That, and all the wars religion has caused. So yeah, stay away from religion."

"Tell me about a time when you were really happy."

"When I realized my God would love me forever unconditionally, and that He knows I will always make mistakes."

"Can you describe what it's like having God in your life?"

"It allows me to relax a bit. I don't get upset when outcomes don't go my way. I realize I'm not in control of these things and maybe God has something even better for me than what I had thought I wanted. So I am able to learn from mistakes and enjoy life as it comes. I'm not in control. And that's ok."

This dog looked completely guilty – glancing left and right for the by-law officer.

Illegal cuteness seen on Baker Street.

HER: "We just moved to Nelson from Australia 10 days ago."

HIM: "This is the first time she's ever touched snow."

"We were living in Oregon. But even in a more left-wing 'blue' state, the polarization of American politics was everywhere. We were just sick of it. And when our kid turned five we actually went travelling around B.C. to a bunch of cities and towns looking for the right school and environment to raise our family. We found the Waldorf school and Nelson. And even though it's not perfect, the issues here are ones I can live with."

"What'd ya get for xmas?"

"Skiiiiiiiiiiiiiiiiiiiiiiiiiiiiiiiiiiiiiiiiiiis!"

These lovely ladies were walking down the street, arm-in-arm with big smiles on their faces. Despite how it might look, I did not pose them one bit.

And our conversation lasted 12 seconds...

SANS TOUQUE: "This is my mom, and my sister."

ME: "And that must make you the centre of the universe."

GREY TOUQUE: "That's about right!"

His English had a thick accent and he had to repeat himself several times. But his excitement came through loud and clear.

"I have a place in Croatia. It's right on the Adriatic Sea. You know there are thousands of kilometers of beautiful shore there. I go visit and travel Europe every year. I just got back three months ago, and I'm going again in... let's see... November or December. I'm 82 and I never miss a year. I just wish I had some company to go with. I would love to show people all the things I've seen – like buildings that are a thousand years old! Just amazing things in Europe that are wonderful."

"Some people think security is more important than quality of life.
But that's not true for me."

"What advice would you give your 21-year-old self?"

"It doesn't matter if you're rich or poor. What matters is you do what you love and you follow your heart. I've had a good life and that's what I've always done."

"I would like to add: The quality of your life does not depend on your circumstances, but on whether you live your life as a privilege or a complaint."

"Did you make that touque yourself?"

"No. But I did make the hole at the top!"

"I grew up in a community that had only 30 houses.
My best friend was my golden retriever."

"I was a vegetarian for four years cause I didn't want to eat my friends. I believe that all life is sacred. But my body wasn't doing well on that diet and I said, 'OK Creator, now what?' I eventually found my way to sacred hunting and fishing. I have cultivated a deep connection with what I eat."

"I want to open up a bakery in Slocan City. I know it's a ghost town, but I love it there."

"That's awesome. I can't wait to taste your bread once you're up and running."

"Dude, where can I find you? I'll bring you a loaf tomorrow. I bake every week and I give it away for free."

"What do you like most about your mom?"

"Her hugs."

I spotted her sitting on the ledge knitting (sorry, crocheting) what she later told me was a mask for a friend. When I asked if I could take a photo of her wearing the mask, she suggested I also get a shot of her incredible tights. "When the mask goes on, the pants come off," she told me—and then proceeded to demonstrate.

Seen on Baker Street.

"Where should we go to get the photo taken?"

HIM: "I could go jump on that cop car."

"Actually, I think right here should be good."

As soon as the owner said her dog was from Mexico,
I immediately and impulsively gave it a Spanish accent.

We talked for nearly an hour. He told me many things, but I wrote down nothing. There was just no pause that would allow it. Plus, I wouldn't have wanted the difficult task of deciding which story to write – and which ones to leave out.

"True happiness comes from within an individual, and exerting yourself in an effort to make someone else happy is not the way to go about it. You need to find the happiness within yourself and radiate that towards everything else."

"I'm travelling across the country and so far I've met some incredible people. This one man took me and my friend into his home in the Okanagan. It was a beautiful place. I was surprised when he gave us a knife and told us to take anything we wanted from the garden. He seemed a bit depressed and lonely, so we decided to cook him dinner. On his birthday we made him a feast. That night he said, 'You have showed me love'. I later found out he entered rehab. I hope he's doing ok."

RIGHT: "I texted her that I was pregnant."

LEFT: "Then I took a pregnancy test that same day and texted her back, 'ME TOO!'"

"You're taking a photograph of an extinct Sinixt Indian."

"I've got a place down in Arizona where we'll ride in the winter."

"There's no helmet law in that state. Do you guys take your helmets off when you're down there?"

"We always ride with our helmets. It's funny, you see women on the back of bikes down there and they're wearing helmets. The guys up front won't be wearing one. It's just stupid."

"Are you guys a couple?"

Looking at each other they both say "Umm..."

"Opps. Sorry. Didn't mean to put you on the spot like that."

HER: "We just met at the hostel. We're both visiting."

HIM: "But I'm moving here."

HER: "Me too."

"One day I counted 168 smiles. 168 smiles! In five hours. No, it was four hours and 45 minutes. I mean, come on, that's pretty awesome. People are just so friendly. A smile means everything to me. Oh look, now I'm gettin' all teared up here."

When I looked back at my notes to see what I was going to write as a caption to this portrait, the words "Stinky Pete" jumped out at me. Now how in the world do you have an eight-minute conversation with a stranger and find out that her family had named a particular dolphin that used to follow their boat up in Haida Gwaii "Stinky Pete"?

"We are all just a combination of atoms on top of a rock. Walking around in our humans suits. I don't know why we take life so seriously."

"Techno music is the artificial drum.

The electric lights and lasers, the artificial fires.

The drugs, the artificial sacred medicine.

And sex without intimacy is artificial love,

artificial true love."

"What does music mean to you?"

"Music is my meditation. My friend says

that music is not entertainment, it's inner-

attainment. "

Seen in Nelson BC.

Izzy on Baker Street.

"I'm in love with a woman who's with another guy. But I found out this morning that she's not with him any more."

"It's freezing out here. Why are you wearing shorts?"

"Because I love shorts."

"I'm from a pioneer family. My great-grandparents built a lot of this town: Hume School, the banks, and many of the old houses – like the ones on Carbonate Street. My great-grandfather arrived here in 1890. He had talent, and put it to good use. A stocky, hard-working Scotsman!"

"And you're still here after all this time. That's amazing."

"There's a few of us still here. But we're like everyone else, you've gotta go where the jobs are. So most of my family has left."

"What keeps you here?"

"I still love this town. It's great to see all the young families here. It balances out the old folks. It's nice to have a mix of young and old. Keeps it fresh and alive, without losing its roots."

"We came to Rossland from France four years ago. Me, my husband and my kids. We were so excited! We didn't have jobs and we didn't even speak English! But it was a love story. It was magical. And we found a way."

"I live in Argenta. I'm in town to do some shopping – and to dance."

"Dance? What kind of dancing do you like to do?"

"Free-style. I don't like being told how to dance or what to dance. With free-style I get to just move to the music any way my body feels like it. It's amazing. You should try it!"

"Someone from work dropped him off at my door. The guy didn't want him, and told me to drop him off at the SPCA if I didn't want him. I thought the dog was ugly at first, with his goggly eyes and crooked tail. And he was a little shit. He crapped on my bed!"

"So why did you keep him?"

"He makes me laugh everyday. I've had him for five years now. He's awesome."

"Regrets? No. I can't really think of any. My psyche is too focused on the positive right now."

"And what's happening that's so positive for you?"

"I just sold my house and I'm running away!"

"Are you running from something or to something?"

"I'm running to something. I am moving to the island where my dream job is waiting for me. I'll be doing research as a music historian. I can't wait!"

"I'm working on being intimate and having a relationship with my whole world – not just one person."

I saw this woman standing under a flower basket at the market, her hair aflame from the evening sun. Unfortunately I lost my notes and what she told me. I believe she was from Australia and she said something like this:

"The thing I miss most about home is the smell – the smell of hot, dusty deserty summers."

Perhaps if everyone I shot gave descriptions like that, I wouldn't need to take notes.

"How did you guys meet?"

"We met on Kijiji. But we weren't on there to find a date. I wanted to do something for myself. And I had always wanted to learn how to play guitar. So I went on Kijiji looking for a guitar teacher. He had an ad. I showed up for my lesson. Then we started dating. It's kinda funny how I was trying to focus on me – but I ended up finding him."

"Tansi! Grandmothers, Grandfathers, spirits of the four directions, I give you thanks for this day! Bless the four-leggeds, two-leggeds, the tall standing people, the sky beings, the rock people and the 13 original rainbow grandmothers! Aho!"

Though I usually save the "what advice would you give your younger self" question for the "older" subjects – I just had to share this answer:

"Travel now, get that degree later, take more risks, don't hold back, don't let go of life's opportunities, stop procrastinating, use more energy on your creativity and start right now, keep practicing that violin, trust your instincts, don't force, don't worry so much and get out of that head, be assertive, speak your mind more often, be more active, sleep more, save more, spend... a little less on beer, knick knacks and damn dresses. Ah bugger it! Do what you want, it is what it is. Don't waste your time on these regrets because you are exactly where you need to be. You are going to turn out just fine and you are going to have a blast!"

"I'm putting a TED Talk together right now. I'm not done, but it's going to be about how the only way we're going to move forward is by working together. What we've been doing for the last 2000 years just isn't working."

"What inspired you to create a presentation for TED?"

"I was working at Burning Man. And it was a gorgeous morning – and there was a good show going on. I remember looking over the crowd and something didn't seem quite right. Then I saw that people were forming these little cliques – these little groups of people. They weren't *together*. And somehow I felt they were missing the point. Burning Man is this progressive event. But I was seeing separation and not togetherness. So that day I decided I would look everyone in the eye and say 'Good morning' to them. Many people were shocked that a stranger would do that. But it brought togetherness. The Good Morning Initiative gets rid of the fear of the Other."

"My dad was very religious. So growing up, Christmas was more about indoctrination than it was about having fun and celebration. I always resented that and wished we could be like other families. But now that I'm older, I'm releasing that resentment and letting go. And I'm also remembering now that it wasn't all bad. Like these Christmas sweaters he would always give us. They were comically hideous! They always made me laugh."

"What's something you're struggling with?"

"Aw man. Life. Me. I can't put my finger on it. That's the problem."

I just happened to run into this nice family on Victoria Street. They were visiting and we were chatting it up, talking about Nelson restaurants. I didn't have my camera out and I wasn't trying to get a photo or anything. Just a nice friendly chat. We talked about the last time they were in Nelson and how they ate at this awesome Thai restaurant.

Suddenly their kid recalled this experience:

"Yeah, the last time we were in Nelson I was in my mom's tummy. I was really warm in there. Then I decided to come out. I opened one eye – and then the other."

I mean, who would have thought a birth story was going to come out of a chat about where to eat while in town?

"When are you the happiest?"

"I have a hard time defining what it means to be happy...
but I guess I'd have to say it's when I'm smoking weed."

As I was trying to get a shot of this dog, he (or she) was being quite fidgety and it was taking a bit of time to get a good shot. This lady must have seen my struggle, and she came over to help us out. You don't see her, but she's just to the left of this frame.

She was talking to the dog and telling it to look my way, and telling me, "There! That's the shot – take it!", but then my focus would go off and I couldn't take the shot.

She tried harder and harder, sometimes waving her hands and arms in front of the lens as she tried to get the dog's attention. It felt like an impossible situation: I had to find a moment where the dog was looking at me, my focus was sharp, and the woman's hands weren't in the frame.

I felt so much pressure to get a great shot for this woman. I hope she sees this post and approves. And I want to thank her for her valiant effort to make it all work. If we all helped each other out with such intensity and passion, the world would be a better place. Thanks, stranger, thanks.

I really like asking kids what their favourite thing about their mom or dad is. You get some great answers. But when I asked this little girl, it didn't feel like she wanted to answer me.

"Are you a bit shy?" I asked her, and I told her about how I'm a bit shy too. And that it's ok to be a bit shy.

She looked at me and smiled a big blueberry & burrito smile and said, "But why are you shy?"

I was kinda speechless. "Why am I shy? Now that's a very good question," I replied.

"Why is that a very good question?"

Ah. I've been in these infinite 'why' conversations before.

Mom and I just looked at each other and smiled.

"You can't tell, but I'm an amputee."

(The photo was taken after our conversation).

"I had an accident. I fell and busted my leg really good. I had a lot of surgeries and it just wasn't getting any better. I was in a lot of pain and I couldn't really do anything – which sucked cause I'm an active guy. So I was thinking about having it amputated. I was thinking about it for nine months and I talked to a few amputees to help me figure out what life would be like if I made that very big decision. 'Cause even though I was in a lot of pain and wasn't getting any better, the idea of only having one leg was a lot to wrap my mind around.

I had my doubts.

And so this one amputee I talked to was telling me it would be a big mistake and that I should continue to fight and keep my leg. In the end, I didn't take his advice. I chose to lose my leg – and it was a great choice. I can now do so much. I longboard, I'm active, and I have a great life ahead of me."

Today in micro-fashion.

Today in micro-fashion.

"What is one of your happiest moments?"

"When I got 100% on my final art project. It was a huge notebook where I wrote about my creative process. The teacher had told the class that no one would get an 'A'. When he returned my notebook, he had written a thank you note inside and told me to get back in touch with him when I was published."

At first it was just him and me:

"What's the happiest moment of your life?"

"This one. Right now. This moment with you."

"Really?"

"Yes. Then in a minute, *that* will be the happiest moment of my life."

"I see."

I took some more photos and literally a minute later, this woman walked down from behind me and embraced this man. They smiled and chatted with each other; obviously they knew one another.

"Did you know she was on her way to see you just now?"

"Nope."

HER: "Before my son was born, my greatest fear was my own death. Now all I can think about is the little or big things that may happen to him."

HIM: "I didn't grow up with a dad. I was in the foster care system. So I don't really have anyone to model as a parent. But I've got age, wisdom, and a wonderful partner. So I know I'll do just fine. Plus, I definitely know what doesn't work, and I'll use that as my guide with him."

"We made $60 busking for an hour and a half!"

"What are you saving up for?"

"I don't know!"

"I'm a non-conformist."

"I kinda play dress up for my five year old self. I do it for her."

"Do you remember your saddest moment?"

"Well, I lost three sons. [long pause] Everyone says I should write a book, but I don't have time."

"I've been living in this tent for the last five months. I'm just fixing the zipper. Doing a bit of spring cleaning of my home, I suppose."

"What was it like to live outdoors during the winter?"

"I've lived in apartments and I always got sick. So living outdoors is where I want to be. But when it's -26 degrees and the night is just getting started and I'm cold, that's when the fears come up. As I lie awake, the cold and the fear become like a meditation. It's just me and my breath. But you know what? I always got through my fears and woke up, opening my tent to the light of day – satisfied and happy. I've learned self-mastery by going into the dark of night alone. After these five months, I have better tolerance of isolation."

"Thanks for talking with me."

"No. Thank you. By saying some of this out loud to you I've just come to realize these things that I've recently gone through. So thank you for listening."

"Politics is my thing. And tango."

"If you could give a piece of advice to a large group of people, what would it be?"

"Don't waste your money away. It takes one poorly spent paycheque to end up where I am."

"I'm 92 years old and I'm from Holland. Sixty years ago I moved to Canada after seeing a picture of Niagara Falls."

"My name is Mike FUNergy"

"Really?"

"No. But yes."

"My dad passed away on Christmas Day two years ago."

"What do you miss the most about him?"

"Honestly? I really miss hanging out at his tattoo shop. Sometimes he'd let me help out – just do little things for him. I thought that what he did was so amazing."

"As a mother, I thought I would be more strict. I mean, my mom was awesome but she didn't exactly know what us kids were getting up to. She was raised on a farm and I was raised in the city."

"Don't all kids think their parents are naive?"

"Maybe, but my mom *really* didn't know. So when I had kids I was probably a little too on top of them. I worried that they were going to try to do the same stuff I did. But they were really good. And I realized pretty soon that I could let them live life and make mistakes. You asked me what my happiest memory is, and it's raising my kids. For sure. And now I can add my grandkids to that too."

"I'm a prospector. So I notice anomalies all around me, things that other people just walk past. Like interesting rocks..." (he reaches down to pick up something off the ground mid-sentence) "...or this nickel."

I have seen this gentleman many times before around town. I used to pass him heading up and down Morgan Street around Gyro bluff. We had never talked until I asked to take his photo on the street.

I told him that I've seen him a lot around town, and I was surprised when he remembered seeing me too. He seemed like one of those guys that knows everyone.

I told him about the Humans of Nelson project. And I've never seen someone be so ecstatic about it. He thought it was just an awesome thing I was doing – taking photos of strangers and posting them online (which sounds weird to say it like that). Anyway, we had this great conversation about it.

In the end, I realized, his excitement and positivity really was more a reflection about who he is, and less about me and this project. And his energy was infectious.

Later on that evening, he passed me while I was shooting another person. I said "hi" and he looked at me and said, "You're just such a great guy."

Does it get any better?

"Last spring I was working and then all of a sudden I was feeling terrible. My whole body got covered in little red dots, my heart rate shot up to 127, and I had trouble breathing. Then I told my boss to touch my tongue – it felt like sandpaper. I was up on the mountain and was airlifted to the hospital. Turns out my blood-glucose level was 26.7, when it should be between four and seven. And that's when I was diagnosed with diabetes. The doctors said I wouldn't have survived a ground transport to the hospital.

Thankfully I can live with this. I just need to have two needles a day – every day,"

"Weren't you upset with the diagnosis?"

"Heck no. It is what it is. And with the needles, I can live a normal life. I appreciate the needles, I appreciate the helicopter."

Unbelievably, these guys sounded even better than they looked.

The dude on the right was rockin' those spoons.

"I went to New York once. I was looking forward to seeing all the wacky people. We all hear how different the folks are out there. So I thought, 'Bring on the crazy!'. And sure, I saw this guy in a skirt playing the harp. But I see that kind of stuff at home on Baker Street too."

"What advice would you give a large group of people?"

"Share love, give love. That may not be the deep
answer you were looking for but it's everything to me."